IMPORTANT-READ CAREFULLY: This End User License Agreement ("Agreement") sets forth the conditions by which Wadsworth, a division of Thomson Learning Inc. ("Thomson") will make electronic access to the Thomson-owned licensed content and associated media, software, documentation, printed materials and electronic documentation contained in this package and/or made available to you via this Website (the "Licensed Content"), available to you (the "End User"). BY CLICKING THE "I ACCEPT" BUTTON AND/OR OPENING THIS PACKAGE, YOU ACKNOWLEDGE THAT YOU HAVE READ ALL OF THE TERMS AND CONDITIONS, AND THAT YOU AGREE TO BE BOUND BY ITS TERMS CONDITIONS AND ALL APPLICABLE LAWS AND REGULATIONS GOVERNING THE USE OF THE LICENSED CONTENT.

1.0 SCOPE OF LICENSE

3.2 <u>Licensed Content</u>. The Licensed Content may contain portions of modifiable content ("Modifiable Content") and content which may not be modified or otherwise altered by the End User ("Non-Modifiable Content"). For purposes of this Agreement, Modifiable Content and Non-Modifiable Content may be collectively referred to herein as the "Licensed Content." All Licensed Content shall be considered Non-Modifiable Content, unless such Licensed Content is presented to the End User in a modifiable format and it is clearly indicated that modification of the Licensed Content is permitted.

3.3 Subject to the End User's compliance with the terms and conditions of this Agreement, Thomson hereby grants the End User, a nontransferable, non-exclusive, limited right to access and view a single copy of the Licensed Content on a single personal computer system for noncommercial, internal, personal use only. The End User shall not (i) reproduce, copy, modify (except in the case of Modifiable Content), distribute, display, transfer, sublicense, prepare derivative work(s) based on, sell, exchange, barter or transfer, rent, lease, loan, resell, or in any other manner exploit the Licensed Content; (ii) remove, obscure or alter any notice of Thomson's intellectual property rights present on or in the License Content, including, but not limited to, copyright, trademark and/or patent notices; or (iii) disassemble, decompile, translate, reverse engineer or otherwise reduce the Licensed Content. Thomson reserves the right to use a hardware lock device, license administration software, and/or a license authorization key to control access or password protection technology to the Licensed Content. The End User may not take any steps to avoid or defeat the purpose of such measures. Use of the Licensed Content without the relevant required lock device or authorization key is prohibited.

2.0 TERMINATION

3.2 Thomson may at any time (without prejudice to its other rights or remedies) immediately terminate this Agreement and/or suspend access to some or all of the Licensed Content, in the event that the End User does not comply with any of the terms and conditions of this Agreement. In the event of such termination by Thomson, the End User shall immediately return any and all copies of the Licensed Content to Thomson.

3.0 PROPRIETARY RIGHTS

3.1 The End User acknowledges that Thomson owns all right, title and interest, including, but not limited to all copyright rights therein, in and to the Licensed Content, and that the End User shall not take any action inconsistent with such ownership. The Licensed Content is protected by U.S., Canadian and other applicable copyright laws and by international treaties, including the Berne Convention and the Universal Copyright Convention. Nothing contained in this Agreement shall be construed as granting the End User any ownership rights in or to the Licensed Content.

3.2 Thomson reserves the right at any time to withdraw from the Licensed Content any item or part of an item for which it no longer retains the right to publish, or which it has reasonable grounds to believe infringes copyright or is defamatory, unlawful or otherwise objectionable.

4.0 PROTECTION AND SECURITY

4.2 The End User shall use its best efforts and take all reasonable steps to safeguard its copy of the Licensed Content to ensure that no unauthorized reproduction, publication, disclosure, modification or distribution of the Licensed Content, in whole or in part, is made. To the extent that the End User becomes aware of any such unauthorized use of the Licensed Content, the End User shall immediately notify Thomson.

5.0 MISUSE OF THE LICENSED PRODUCT

5.2 In the event that the End User uses the Licensed Content in violation of this Agreement, Thomson shall have the option of electing liquidated damages, which shall include all profits generated by the End User's use of the Licensed Content plus interest computed at the maximum rate permitted by law and all legal fees and other expenses incurred by Thomson in enforcing its rights, plus penalties.

6.0 FEDERAL GOVERNMENT CLIENTS

6.2 Except as expressly authorized by Thomson, Federal Government clients obtain only the rights specified in this Agreement and no other rights. The Government acknowledges that (i) all software and related documentation incorporated in the Licensed Content is existing commercial computer software within the meaning of FAR 27.405(b)(2); and (2) all other data delivered in whatever form, is limited rights data within the meaning of FAR 27.401. The restrictions in this section are acceptable as consistent with the Government's need for software and other data under this Agreement.

7.0 DISCLAIMER OF WARRANTIES AND LIABILITIES

7.2 Although Thomson believes the Licensed Content to be reliable, Thomson does not guarantee or warrant (i) any information or materials contained in or produced by the Licensed Content, (ii) the accuracy, completeness or reliability of the Licensed Content, or (iii) that the Licensed Content is free from errors or other material defects. THE LICENSED PRODUCT IS PROVIDED "AS IS," WITHOUT ANY WARRANTY OF ANY KIND AND THOMSON DISCLAIMS ANY AND ALL WARRANTIES, EXPRESSED OR IMPLIED, INCLUDING, WITHOUT LIMITATION, WARRANTIES OF MERCHANTABILITY OR FITNESS OR A PARTICULAR PURPOSE. IN NO EVENT SHALL THOMSON BE LIABLE FOR: INDIRECT, SPECIAL, PUNITIVE OR CONSEQUENTIAL DAMAGES INCLUDING FOR LOST PROFITS, LOST DATA, OR OTHERWISE. IN NO EVENT SHALL THOMSON'S AGGREGATE LIABILITY HEREUNDER, WHETHER ARISING IN CONTRACT, TORT, STRICT LIABILITY OR OTHERWISE, EXCEED THE AMOUNT OF FEES PAID BY THE END USER HEREUNDER FOR THE LICENSE OF THE LICENSED CONTENT.

8.0 GENERAL

8.2 Entire Agreement. This Agreement shall constitute the entire Agreement between the Parties and supercedes all prior Agreements and understandings oral or written relating to the subject matter hereof.

8.3 Enhancements/Modifications of Licensed Content. From time to time, and in Thomson's sole discretion, Thomson may advise the End User of updates, upgrades, enhancements and/or improvements to the Licensed Content, and may permit the End User to access and use, subject to the terms and conditions of this Agreement, such modifications, upon payment of prices as may be established by Thomson.

8.4 No Export. The End User shall use the Licensed Content solely in the United States and shall not transfer or export, directly or indirectly, the Licensed Content outside the United States.

8.5 Severability. If any provision of this Agreement is invalid, illegal, or unenforceable under any applicable statute or rule of law, the provision shall be deemed omitted to the extent that it is invalid, illegal, or unenforceable. In such a case, the remainder of the Agreement shall be construed in a manner as to give greatest effect to the original intention of the parties hereto.

8.6 Waiver. The waiver of any right or failure of either party to exercise in any respect any right provided in this Agreement in any instance shall not be deemed to be a waiver of such right in the future or a waiver of any other right under this Agreement.

8.7 Choice of Law/Venue. This Agreement shall be interpreted, construed, and governed by and in accordance with the laws of the State of New York, applicable to contracts executed and to be wholly preformed therein, without regard to its principles governing conflicts of law. Each party agrees that any proceeding arising out of or relating to this Agreement or the breach or threatened breach of this Agreement may be commenced and prosecuted in a court in the State and County of New York. Each party consents and submits to the non-exclusive personal jurisdiction of any court in the State and County of New York in respect of any such proceeding.

3.1 Acknowledgment. By opening this package and/or by accessing the Licensed Content on this Website, THE END USER ACKNOWLEDGES THAT IT HAS READ THIS AGREEMENT, UNDERSTANDS IT, AND AGREES TO BE BOUND BY ITS TERMS AND CONDITIONS. IF YOU DO NOT ACCEPT THESE TERMS AND CONDITIONS, YOU MUST NOT ACCESS THE LICENSED CONTENT AND RETURN THE LICENSED PRODUCT TO THOMSON (WITHIN 30 CALENDAR DAYS OF THE END USER'S PURCHASE) WITH PROOF OF PAYMENT ACCEPTABLE TO THOMSON, FOR A CREDIT OR A REFUND. Should the End User have any questions/comments regarding this Agreement, please contact Thomson at tl.support@thomson.com.

ABC News
BIOLOGY IN THE HEADLINES
2006 on DVD

Edited by:
Jane A. Willan

THOMSON
BROOKS/COLE

Australia • Brazil • Canada • Mexico • Singapore • Spain • United Kingdom • United States

© 2007 Thomson Brooks/Cole, a part of The Thomson Corporation. Thomson, the Star logo, and Brooks/Cole are trademarks used herein under license.

ALL RIGHTS RESERVED. No part of this work covered by the copyright hereon may be reproduced or used in any form or by any means—graphic, electronic, or mechanical, including photocopying, recording, taping, Web distribution, information storage and retrieval systems, or in any other manner—except as may be permitted by the license terms herein.

Printed in the United States of America

1 2 3 4 5 6 7 11 10 09 08 07

Printer: ePAC

ISBN-13: 978-0-495-01602-1
ISBN-10: 0-495-01602-0

For more information about our products, contact us at:
**Thomson Learning Academic Resource Center
1-800-423-0563**

For permission to use material from this text or product, submit a request online at
http://www.thomsonrights.com.
Any additional questions about permissions can be submitted by email to **thomsonrights@thomson.com.**

**Thomson Higher Education
10 Davis Drive
Belmont, CA 94002-3098
USA**

SEGMENT TITLES AND DESCRIPTIONS

1. FOOD ALLERGY INCREASE (4:54)

Following the dramatic death of one Canadian teenager as a result of a peanut allergy reaction, people are asking whether food allergies are becoming more deadly. The number of American children with nut allergies has doubled in the last several years. Americans have the highest incidence of peanut allergies. Researchers suggest that this is because Americans eat a high quantity of dry-roasted peanuts. The dry-roasting process changes the structure of the protein that causes the allergic reaction. Another theory states that American children in particular are too clean for their own good. The lack of exposure to a variety of germs and allergens at an early age has caused the immune system to overreact to specific foods, increasing the rate of allergic reactions. An estimated 1.5 million Americans have a peanut allergy, considered the most deadly of all food allergies. Each year it is estimated that 50 to 100 people die from a peanut allergy reaction. Peanut allergy reactions from kissing are thought to be 5 percent of reactions. People who are most allergic to peanuts should be vigilant about their environments. Since this is often difficult, they can also be proactive and carry an "epi-pen," which is a pen syringe that can be used to inject a dose of epinephrine at the first sign of a reaction. This allows the sufferer time to call for assistance or get to an emergency room for further treatment.

2. FAT MAN WALKING (1:31)

In a drastic effort to regain his health and happiness, Californian Steve Vaught set out on a walk across the United States by way of Historic Route 66. He left his home in Oceanside, California, weighing 410 pounds (186 kilograms), and arrived in New York City—3000 miles (4830 kilometers) and one year and one month later—weighing about 100 pounds (45 kilograms) lighter. Steve started his journey with the goal in mind to change his behavior and eating habits rather than just to lose weight. He also used his journey to alleviate the severe depression he had been suffering for fifteen years after accidentally killing two elderly pedestrians. He chronicled his trip on his Internet blog. While walking, he went through 15 pairs of shoes, more than 30 pairs of socks, and 6 backpacks. He slept in a tent or at motels along his route.

3. INDONESIAN EARTHQUAKE (2:02)

On May 27, 2006, a 6.2 earthquake shook awake many people in the region surrounding the ancient city of Yogyakarta. The earthquake flattened many buildings in central Indonesia and killed at least 2,500 people. Approximately two-thirds of the deaths were in the district of Bantul, considered the worst-hit by the earthquake. It was the worst natural disaster since the 2004 Indian Ocean tsunami. Fearful of a recurrence, thousands of survivors headed immediately for higher ground. There were so many injured that Yogyakarta hospital personnel had to treat people outside and on the floors of the hospitals. Residents began to bury their dead as soon after the disaster as possible, often with other survivors looking on while taking refuge in the open space of the cemeteries. The earthquake also triggered heightened activity in the nearby active Mount Merapi volcano.

4. ATLANTIC STATES FLOODING (1:34)

Record rains in the northeastern United States during the spring of 2006 resulted in widespread flooding. In the state of Maryland, thousands of people were evacuated from their homes, especially those along creeks and rivers. Two Maryland youths were reported missing after being caught in the fast moving river water. Around Lake Needwood, about 2,200 people were evacuated as the lake rose to almost 25 feet (7.5 meters) above normal. The lake's earthen dam was also weakened in a number of spots, with officials estimating that a dam break would cause flooding up to 20 feet (6.0 meters) in some areas. Residents in parts of New Jersey, New York, and Pennsylvania were also ordered to evacuate. The weather was caused by a low-pressure system that stalled off the East Coast for several days and pushed moist tropical air north.

5. HUMAN ZOO (2:50)

As part of the Urban Dream Capsule (UDC), an extended performance art event, four Australian actors created a "human zoo" in downtown Shanghai, China. These four actors lived behind the glass windows of an empty storefront, leaving the windows completely open for the entire performance time of twelve days. The actors picked an active area of the trendy Xintiandi district in Shanghai. Despite the obvious glass barrier, the event was highly interactive with participants and spectators communicating through body language, verbally through the glass, and by telephone and written communication, including email, fax, and paper. The actors encouraged spectators to stop by dancing, performing skits, or merely allowing them to observe otherwise private moments. Spectators were also able to see participants washing up. Chinese onlookers commented that they enjoyed seeing the Australian actors, seeing how they lived and interacted with each other, and practicing their English language skills. The performers were under non-stop public scrutiny.

6. TSUNAMI ALERT TESTING (3:24)

In response to the 2004 Indian Ocean tsunami, an early alert warning system has been developed and tested. More than two dozen Pacific Rim nations participated in a tsunami drill during May of 2006. Thousands of residents of countries, including the Philippines, El Salvador, Chile, China, and the U.S. Hawaiian Islands, responded to the drill's alert, reacting as they would during a real disaster. The director of the Pacific Tsunami Warning Center in Hawaii stated that the warning system had been in place for 40 years, but this is the first time a drill has taken place. The fictitious earthquake registered at 9.2 on the Richter scale, and the tsunami wave grew to 30 feet (10 meters) in height.

7. CAHUACHI EXCAVATION (2:00)

Archaeologists continue to unveil the new artifacts uncovered each year from the excavation of the Temple of Cahuachi, which is an ancient site and assumed ceremonial center of the Nazca culture of Peru. Giuseppe Orefici, an Italian archaeologist who has been excavating the Temple for the last several decades, made the most recent presentation of new artifacts. In addition to unearthing artifacts, the archaeologists work to preserve a dominating 98-foot high pyramid that is similar in shape to the Aztec pyramids and to unearth other structures reinforced by adobe. These other structures are assumed to be either smaller temples or visiting rooms for pilgrims to the site, as they do not contain living rooms or bedrooms. The Temple is thought to have been built in approximately 5000 BC, before the Nazca culture. The 24-square-kilometer area of adobe structures is found near the Nazca Lines in the Peruvian desert, which consist of some 300 figures of straight lines and geometric shapes that are most clearly seen from the air.

8. OHIO FLOODING (1:14)

A long and consistent line of severe storm systems during July 2006 caused widespread flooding and damage in Ohio. In addition to the large amount of rainfall from the storms, tornadoes were also reported to have caused damage. Lake County, in particular, experienced heavy damage. Governor Bob Taft declared the county in a state of emergency. The declaration allowed the state to assist in rescue and cleanup efforts. Many area residents were forced to flee their homes as ten inches of rain caused the Grand River to reach eleven feet above flood level. One Eastlake, Ohio, man was reported missing near the Chagrin River.

9. MULE CLONES WIN QUALIFYING HEATS (2:39)

In the first competitive race that included cloned animals, two identical mule clones were raced at the 20th Annual Winnemucca Mule race in Winnemucca, Nevada. Mules are typically the sterile offspring of a horse mother and a donkey father. The two cloned mules covered the 350-yard track to win their individual qualifying heats—Idaho Gem clocking in at 21.817 seconds and Idaho Star in at 21.790 seconds—respectively beating out five and four other rivals. Donald Jacklin of the American Mule Racing Association and financier of the cloning project highly supports the project, stating that these winners would encourage other people to consider the positive benefits of cloning. The cloned mules' original DNA was taken from a fetus produced by the same parents who sired a champion mule racer. Idaho Gem and Idaho Star were separated in their second year and raised and trained independently. Scientists hope to use the data from their racing careers to study the affects of nature versus nurture.

10. GLOW-IN-THE-DARK PIGS (1:36)

Taiwanese scientists at Taiwan University claim to have successfully bred transgenic pigs that are green in color and can glow in the dark. There have been partially green pigs before, but these pigs are the first to be green from the inside out, including their heart and other internal organs. These pigs are transgenic because they have been developed by taking genes from a different animal and inserting them into the genes of an embryonic pig. To make these green pigs, Taiwanese scientists extracted green protein from a jellyfish and injected the gene for the protein into embryonic pig cells. After the embryo grows and becomes a pig, it is fluorescent and glows in the dark, though only one in a hundred attempts produces a successfully mature green pig. Scientists expect to use this research to benefit the study of human diseases.

11. SEA TURTLE RELEASE (1:17)

As part of United Nations (UN) Environment Day program, endangered breeds of sea turtles, including the Carey, Green, and Caguana, were released back into the Caribbean Sea. The turtles had either been bred and raised in captivity or were captured by local fishermen and rehabilitated. The UN intended this program to promote global awareness of the environment and encourage political action. The turtle release in Colombia was specifically aimed at raising global awareness of the plight of the sea turtles. The program also trained local fishermen and indigenous communities to care for captured turtles. This program was designed to reduce the number of exotic animals smuggled from Colombia to the United States, Europe, and Asia each year. This smuggling typically results in the death of these animals, which contributes to the extinction of exotic species such as parrots, other tropical birds, and frogs.

12. ANCIENT HUMAN SKULL (2:04)

Georgian anthropologists and archeologists have found what is believed to be the oldest human remains in Europe outside the village of Dmanisi, southeast of the Georgian capital, Tbilisi. Though Georgia is south of the Caucasus Mountains, east of the Black Sea, and northeast of Turkey, it is geographically considered a part of Europe. The skull is estimated to be 1.8 million years old and is the oldest remains found outside of Africa. The large number of archaeological findings in eastern Georgia has attracted a lot of attention since the early 1900s. These sites provide a large amount of information about early humans, and the numerous finds indicate a primitive human settlement in this region. They also indicate that humans might have left Africa a half million years earlier than previously thought. Further study of the skull will help scientists determine which species of human remains are at this site—*Homo erectus* or *Homo habilis*, what physical features enabled them to leave Africa, and how their bodies and tool usage allowed them to move more freely.

13. MOUNT MERAPI VOLCANO ERUPTION (1:56)

Forty-five hundred people were evacuated in Indonesia in May 2006, following heightened activity in the Mount Merapi volcano. Volcanic ash covered the rooftops of area houses, and children wore masks to protect themselves. The last time the volcano erupted was in 1994 when about 60 people burned to death. Mount Merapi is one of 129 active volcanoes in Indonesia and is located on the densely populated Java Island. One eruption sent an avalanche of debris and ash down the western slope for 2.5 miles (4 kilometers). These types of eruptions are most threatening to the farmers who live on the volcano's slopes and farm the rich volcanic soils that produce bumper crops each year.

14. SECOND-CHANCE HEART (3:30)

A southern Wales girl, Hannah Clark, had a donor heart removed after her own diseased heart became strong enough to function again. Doctors initially added the second heart, to "piggyback" on her diseased heart, ten years prior when Hannah was first diagnosed with cardiomyopathy—a condition which meant her heart was inflamed to twice its size and too weak to pump her blood. The decision to remove her second heart was made after she started having serious complications with her immune system due to the immune suppression drugs she took to keep her body from rejecting the donor heart. The whole procedure took less than four hours and Hannah was home in southern Wales within five days. Hannah stated that following the removal of her second heart, she felt empty on the inside. Doctors were excited about the success of the operation, as it could lead to new treatments for other patients with diseased and failing organs. Hannah's long-term prognosis is unknown as her condition is unique, perhaps the first of its type in the world.

15. REGENERATIVE HUMAN ORGANS (5:39)

Scientists have made a major breakthrough in human transplant technology. For the first time, a complex human organ has been grown in a laboratory and transplanted into a human patient. Dr. Anthony Atala, director of the Institute for Regenerative Medicine at Wake Forest University, has spent the last sixteen years working on regenerating human cells and organs. For one patient, Dr. Atala grew a new bladder, using tissue samples from the diseased organ. These were then placed on a biodegradable mold of a healthy bladder and seeded with the patient's own stem cells. By using the patient's own stem cells, many of the common side effects of transplantation, including immuno-suppression drugs and organ rejection, can be avoided. Other organs currently being researched for regenerative growth include heart valves, blood vessels, and nearly two dozen others. For millions of Americans waiting for new organs, this new technology could mean a wait of months, rather than years, for a donor organ match.

16. NEW SPECIES FOUND (2:43)

During a December 2005 expedition into Papua, New Guinea's Foja Mountains, scientists discovered a plethora of new species. The expedition was a joint project between United States-based Conservation International and the Indonesian Institute of Sciences. The Foja Mountains cover a region of more than a million hectares of old-growth tropical forest. Access to this remote wildlife sanctuary by foreigners is highly restricted due to a decades-long separatist rebellion in the region that has left an estimated 100,000 people dead. These new discoveries included twenty frog species, four types of butterflies, five types of palms, as well as some larger animals that have been hunted to near extinction in other regions, such as the golden-mantled tree kangaroo, the six-wired bird of paradise, and a new honeyeater bird. The lack of human impact on the area gives scientists a view of what the region was like 50,000 years ago.

Name_____ Class_____ Section_____

FOOD ALLERGY INCREASE   **WORKSHEET 1**

Answer the following.

1. What event caused people to question the rate of food allergies?

2. Which nationality has the highest incidence of peanut allergies?

3. List two possible reasons why so many Americans have peanut allergies.

4. Why is this issue so concerning?

5. What precautions can people who are allergic to peanuts take?

Name_____ Class_____ Section_____

FAT MAN WALKING **WORKSHEET 2**

Answer the following.

1. List Steve's beginning and ending weights and calculate his total weight loss.

2. In addition to weight loss, what were Steve's other goals?

3. What type and how much equipment did Steve have? What other equipment do you think he might have needed?

4. It is estimated that 16 percent of Americans suffer from depression at some point in their lives. Do you think that exercise can help their suffering? Explain your answer.

5. There are a large number of books about people walking across the United States. Would you walk across the U.S. or another country? Why would you make the journey—health, happiness, vacation, to raise money, or to raise awareness? What route would you take? Explain your answer.

Name_____ Class_____ Section_____

INDONESIAN EARTHQUAKE   **WORKSHEET 3**

Answer the following.

1. What was the magnitude of the May 27th Indonesian earthquake?

2. What was the major city in Indonesia that was impacted by the earthquake?

3. What happened to the city and the people? List some of the consequences of the earthquake.

4. In addition to the city and people, what geological features were affected by the earthquake?

5. What was one of the first activities most Indonesians undertook after the earthquake was over?

Name_____ Class_____ Section_____

ATLANTIC STATES FLOODING **WORKSHEET 4**

Answer the following.

1. What caused the record rains during the spring of 2006 along the East Coast?

2. What effect did the rains have on the region?

3. In Lake Needwood, Maryland, waters rose to what height?

4. List the other states that had to order residents to evacuate.

5. Speculate on what type of damage can occur after a dam breaks. Can it trigger other natural disasters? Explain your answer.

Name_____ Class_____ Section_____

HUMAN ZOO WORKSHEET 5

Answer the following.

1. What location did the performers use for their event? Explain why this was a good location.

2. What activities did the performers engage in to attract the attention of their audience?

3. What type of communication did the performers and audience engage in?

4. What type of non-verbal communication do you suppose the performers and spectators used to overcome any language barriers? List possibilities and explain your answers.

5. Why is this type of exhibition potentially very beneficial for relations between different cultures? Would you participate in an event like this? Explain your answers, particularly noting if you would participate as a performer or spectator and why.

Name_____ Class_____ Section_____

TSUNAMI ALERT TESTING   **WORKSHEET 6**

Answer the following.

1. This tsunami drill was in direct response to which natural disaster?

2. How many countries, in which region of the globe, participated in the drill?

3. List some of the countries where citizens reacted to the drill.

4. During the drill, false reports were sent out to simulate the real occurrence of both an earthquake and the resulting tsunami. What were the numbers that each event registered on their respective scales?

5. Why, in your opinion, was this the first time a drill has been performed despite the fact that the system has been in place for over 40 years? Be sure to fully explain your answer.

Name_____ Class_____ Section_____

CAHUACHI EXCAVATION   **WORKSHEET 7**

Answer the following.

1. For what ancient culture was Cahuachi presumed a major religious site? In which modern-day country is Cahuachi?

2. What was the time period during which the Cahuachi temple is presumed to have been built?

3. What elements do the smaller structures lack that suggest they were small temples or visiting rooms for pilgrims?

4. What indicators exist to suggest that the Temple with its surrounding structures was a pilgrimage site?

5. What activities do you think might have been performed at the Temple? Explain your answer(s).

Name_____ Class_____ Section_____

OHIO FLOODING **WORKSHEET 8**

Answer the following.

1. How much rain fell in the Lake County area of Ohio?

2. And how much did this raise the level of the Grand River?

3. What was the consequence of Governor Taft's state of emergency declaration?

4. List the different types of damage that could be caused by these storms.

Name_____ Class_____ Section_____

MULE CLONES WIN QUALIFYING HEATS   WORKSHEET 9

Answer the following.

1. Explain the factors necessary to term an animal a mule.

2. Why are Idaho Gem and Idaho Star considered special?

3. Donald Jacklin, supporter of the cloning project, says that this will open people's eyes to the benefits of cloning. What would you consider to be some of the benefits?

4. Scientists will study the data produced by Idaho Star and Idaho Gem's racing careers. Why is this information important to society in general? Explain your answer.

5. How do you feel about cloning animals? What are the advantages and disadvantages of this scientific field? Elaborate on your position.

Name_____ Class_____ Section_____

GLOW-IN-THE-DARK PIGS WORKSHEET 10

Answer the following.

1. What claim are scientists at Taiwan University making?

2. List the steps Taiwanese scientists took to achieve this result.

3. Speculate on how this type of research can assist scientists in studying human diseases and in stem cell research.

4. This type of research can be considered controversial. How so and why would people argue for or against transgenic research? Explain your view of the consequences that could result from this research.

Name_____ Class_____ Section_____

SEA TURTLE RELEASE   **WORKSHEET 11**

Answer the following.

1. What is the United Nations Environment Day program designed to do?

2. In Colombia, part of this program was specifically intended to do what?

3. Some of the released turtles had not been bred and raised in captivity. Where were these turtles found? What did the release of these turtles teach?

4. In addition to endangered turtles of the Caribbean, the UN program was intended to raise awareness of the plight of other native species. What other Colombian species concern the UN? Explain what their specific plight is.

5. What steps do you think could be taken in addition to the United Nations Environment Day program to discourage harm to endangered species and smuggling of exotic animals?

Name_____ Class_____ Section_____

ANCIENT HUMAN SKULL   **WORKSHEET 12**

Answer the following.

1. Georgia is geographically considered part of Europe, though perhaps not politically. List the geographical features that help reinforce this political separation.

2. What is the estimated age of the Georgian skull? Why is this skull important?

3. Why are the Georgian excavations important? With what type of information do they provide scientists?

4. What do scientists hope to learn from further study of the Georgian skull?

Name_____ Class_____ Section_____

MOUNT MERAPI VOLCANO ERUPTION   **WORKSHEET 13**

Answer the following.

1. How many people were evacuated from the area near Mount Merapi after its activity increased?

2. Give an example of one eruption from Mount Merapi.

3. How many active volcanoes are there in Indonesia?

4. Why might people decide to live on the slopes of an active volcano?

5. What is at least one precautionary measure that residents could take? What would cause them to take this precaution?

Name_____ Class_____ Section_____

SECOND-CHANCE HEART WORKSHEET 14

Answer the following.

1. What condition did Hannah Clark suffer from? What effects did the condition cause?

2. To remedy her situation, what did doctors originally do?

3. What happened to cause doctors to decide to remove the donor (second) heart?

4. How could the success of Hannah's operations and treatment benefit society in general?

5. In your opinion, could there be psychologically consequences to this type of treatment?

Name_____ Class_____ Section_____

REGENERATIVE HUMAN ORGANS   **WORKSHEET 15**

Answer the following.

1. Why is Dr. Atala researching the regenerative capabilities of human organs?

2. What tissues must Dr. Atala use to regenerate a human organ?

3. How does this new process improve the transplant procedure?

4. What does this mean to society in general? Explain your answer.

5. Currently, there is a big debate over stem cell research. Dr. Atala uses the patient's own stem cells. How is this different from the stem cells referred to in the national debate? Do you agree with Dr. Atala's research? Explain your reasoning.

Name_____ Class_____ Section_____

NEW SPECIES FOUND   **WORKSHEET 16**

Answer the following.

1. What is the name of the mountain range the expedition team explored? List also the region and country the mountain range is located in.

2. What organizations sponsored the expedition team?

3. List the types of new species found by the expedition team.

4. Why were scientists able to find all of these news species in Papua?

5. Speculate about what your region would look like if humans did not live there. Use plenty of details to explain your answer.

ANSWER KEY

FOOD ALLERGY INCREASE

1. A Canadian teenager with a peanut allergy died after she kissed her boyfriend who had eaten a peanut butter sandwich several hours before. This event has caused many people to consider the rate of allergic reactions to various foods.

2. Americans are the largest group with peanut allergies.

3. One reason is the amount of dry-roasted peanuts Americans consume each year. Dry roasting the peanut causes a change in the protein that triggers the allergic reaction. Another reason is the lack of exposure young American children have to a variety of germs. It is thought that this lack of exposure can cause the immune system to overreact to certain foods.

4. Peanut allergies are considered the most deadly of all food allergies. It is thought that between 50 and 100 people die each year from peanut allergies.

5. They can be cautious about their home environment and in allowing peanuts and other nuts into the house. In outside environments, they must be vigilant about cross-contamination in restaurant foods and what they choose to eat. They can also carry an "epi-pen"—a syringe with epinephrine in it.

FAT MAN WALKING

1. Beginning weight: 410 pounds; ending weight: approximately 310 pounds; total weight loss: 100 pounds

2. He wanted to find happiness, alleviate his depression, and change his behavior and eating habits.

3. Answers will vary, but should include: 15 pairs of shoes, more than 30 pairs of socks, 6 backpacks, and a tent. Answers may also include: books, alarm clock, raincoat, snow gear, matches, dried food, and a large supply of water.

4. Answers will vary.

5. Answers will vary.

INDONESIAN EARTHQUAKE

1. The magnitude was 6.2 on the Richter scale.
2. Yogyakarta is the major city in Indonesia that bore the brunt of the earthquake.
3. Many buildings in the region were flattened, a large number of people were injured, at least 2,500 were killed, people fled to higher ground for fear of a tsunami, and hospital personnel had to treat patients outdoors and on hospital floors.
4. The earthquake caused heightened activity in the active Mount Merapi volcano.
5. Many residents and survivors buried their dead family members and relatives.

ATLANTIC STATES FLOODING

1. A low-pressure storm system stalled off the East Coast for several days caused a lot of tropical rain to be pushed north where it cooled and came down as rain in more than usual amounts.
2. Because there was so much more rain than usual, it filled lakes and rivers to capacity and beyond, resulting in widespread flooding. Many people were evacuated because of the threat of flooding. The large amount of water also weakened area dams.
3. The waters in Lake Needwood rose to almost 25 feet above normal.
4. New Jersey, New York, and Pennsylvania
5. Answers will vary, but may include various types of damage to personal and commercial property, soil contamination/devastation, and crop loss.

HUMAN ZOO

1. They used an empty storefront in the trendy Xintiandi district, in downtown Shanghai, China. This was a good location because a large number of people pass through this area and that allowed more interaction with the audience.
2. Activities listed may vary, but could include: performing skits, dancing, and private activities, such as writing letters and reading.
3. They used various means of communication, including paper, phone, fax, email, body language, and verbal communication through the glass.
4. Answers will vary.
5. Answers will vary.

TSUNAMI ALERT TESTING

1. It was in response to the 2004 Indian Ocean tsunami.
2. Over two dozen countries participated in the drill, along the Pacific Rim coast.
3. Philippines, El Salvador, Chile, China, and the United States are all possible answers.
4. The earthquake registered 9.2 on the Richter scale, and the tsunami wave was to reach 30 feet in height.
5. Answers will vary.

CAHUACHI EXCAVATION

1. Cahuachi was important to the ancient Nazca culture of modern-day Peru.
2. The Temple of Cahuachi is thought to have been built in 5000 BC, predating the Nazca culture.
3. They lack living and sleeping spaces necessary for permanent residents.
4. Cahuachi is located near the Nazca Lines in the Peruvian desert. The Nazca Lines show creatures such as orca and monkeys, which were not present in the Nazca region.
5. Answers will vary, but could include: religious ceremonies, sacrificial ceremonies, and worship.

OHIO FLOODING

1. Ten inches of rain fell.
2. Those ten inches raised the river level to eleven feet above flood level.
3. As a result of his declaration, the state government was able to lend aid to the county with rescue and cleanup efforts.
4. Answers will vary, but could include: flood damage, mold, tornado or wind damage, damage to personal property, loss of possessions, and water damage.

MULE CLONES WIN QUALIFYING HEATS

1. An animal is classed as a mule when it is the offspring of a donkey father and a horse mother. It is usually a sterile animal.
2. They are the first identical cloned mules. They are also the first cloned animals to compete in a competitive race and to have won.
3. Answers will vary, but could include: a healthier animal, a less injury-prone animal, and use of cloning to retain the desirable traits of a particular mule, since they are typically sterile.
4. Idaho Gem and Idaho Star were separated during their second year to be raised and trained independent of each other. This information will allow scientists to see how different environments can affect the development and productive capacity of an identical being—nurture versus nature.
5. Answers will vary.

GLOW-IN-THE-DARK PIGS

1. They claim to have developed the first breed of pig that is green internally and externally and that can glow in the dark.
2. Extract green protein from a jellyfish; inject gene from protein into embryonic pig cells; allow embryo to develop into mature pig; only one in a hundred pigs is successfully green.
3. Answers will vary, but may include: fluorescent organs of the pigs will allow researchers to identify and to extract useful tissues and genes more easily; fluorescent cells will show up during stem cell treatment of diseased organs.
4. Answers will vary.

SEA TURTLE RELEASE

1. It promotes global awareness of the environment and encourages people to take political action to reverse the damage to the environment.
2. To raise global awareness of the plight of endangered sea turtles
3. Local fishermen had captured them. They were rehabilitated and released. Releasing these turtles taught the local, indigenous communities to care for the exotic species native to their region of Colombia.
4. The plight of parrots, other tropical birds, and frogs concerns the UN. Smuggling often causes death and results in further extinction of these species.
5. Answers will vary.

ANCIENT HUMAN SKULL

1. These geographical features include being south of the Caucasus Mountains, east of the Black Sea, and northeast of Turkey.
2. Scientists estimate that it is 1.8 million years old. It is thought to be the oldest human remains in Europe. Its age indicates that humans left Africa a half million years earlier than previously thought.
3. They are important because they provide information about early humans and their settlements.
4. Scientists hope that further study of the skull will determine if the skull belongs to the *Homo erectus* or *Homo habilis* species, what physical features allowed humans to leave Africa, and how their bodies and tool usage allowed them more freedom of movement.

MOUNT MERAPI VOLCANO ERUPTION

1. The Indonesian authorities evacuated 4,500 people.
2. One example is the avalanche of debris and ash on the western slope that traveled for 2.5 miles.
3. Indonesia has 129 active volcanoes.
4. The rich volcanic soils located there produce a bumper crop each year, when not destroyed by volcanic activity.
5. Answers will vary, but could include: wearing masks to protect themselves from the volcanic ash in the air.

SECOND-CHANCE HEART

1. Hannah suffered from cardiomyopathy. It caused her heart to inflame to twice its original size and was too weak to pump her blood.
2. To help Hannah's weak heart, doctors transplanted a second heart to "piggyback" on her diseased heart.
3. Hannah developed severe complications with her immune system from her immune suppression medication. Doctors realized that her own heart must have recovered and was beginning to function properly again—making the donor heart unnecessary.
4. Answers will vary; however, should include something similar to: Other patients with failing and diseased organs could potentially also seek a form of "piggyback" treatment, where a second donor organ could be incorporated into the patient's body until the diseased organ recovers and can function properly again.
5. Answers will vary.

REGENERATIVE HUMAN ORGANS

1. Using a patient's own stem cells reduces the risk of certain side effects—potential rejection of replacement or repaired organs—and allows the patient to heal themselves.
2. Dr. Atala must use the patient's own stem cells to successfully encourage regeneration of a patient's organ.
3. In the case of bladder repair, this method uses stem cells that will mimic the type of cells that make up the bladder, whose primary function is to secrete, rather than repairing the bladder with intestinal tissue, whose primary function is to absorb.
4. Americans suffering from bladder disease might be able to use this new technique to essentially heal themselves. This technique is also being used to grow new heart valves, blood vessels, and almost two dozen other human organs.
5. Answers will vary.

NEW SPECIES FOUND

1. The team explored the Foja Mountains in Papua, New Guinea.
2. The team was made up of scientists from U.S.-based Conservation International and the Indonesian Institute of Sciences.
3. The expedition team found twenty frog species, four types of butterflies, five types of palms, the golden-mantled tree kangaroo, the six-wired bird of paradise, and a honeyeater bird.
4. It is a remote region that has restricted access to foreigners due to decades-old political strife. It is also classified as a wildlife sanctuary. The impact of human life on this region has been limited, so many species were not hunted to extinction.
5. Answers will vary.